THE **TESTING** SERIES

HOW TO
WRITE
A CV

THE **TESTING** SERIES
expert advice on test preparation

how2become

Orders: Please contact How2become Ltd,
Suite 2, 50 Churchill Square Business Centre, Kings Hill, Kent ME19 4YU.

You can also order via the e mail address info@how2become.co.uk.

First published 2012. ISBN: 9781909229976

Printed in Great Britain for How2become Ltd
by Bell & Bain Ltd, 303 Burnfield Road, Thornliebank, Glasgow G46 7UQ

CONTENTS

PREFACE   **VII**

CHAPTER 1
HOW TO WRITE A CV   **1**

CHAPTER 2
CV SAMPLES   **17**
    SAMPLE 1   **18**
    SAMPLE 2   **21**
    SAMPLE 3   **24**
    SAMPLE 4   **27**
    SAMPLE 5   **30**
    SAMPLE 6   **32**

CHAPTER 3
STEP-BY-STEP GUIDE TO WRITING A CV   **35**

CHAPTER 4
FURTHER TIPS FOR CREATING YOUR CV   **43**

Get FREE access to an online CV writing video and templates at:

www.CVwritingSkills.co.uk

PREFACE
BY RICHARD MCMUNN

My name is Richard McMunn and over the years I have helped hundreds of people to find work through my website how2become.com. I have developed a simple to follow, step-by-step process for creating CV's that really do work! Within this workbook I will share with you my CV creating process, tips and advice and strategies for getting past the initial stage of any job selection process.

The workbook, as you will see, is relatively short in length; this is intentional. I see absolutely no reason to create a CV book that is a few hundred pages long; simply because I do not need that much space to teach you something that is relatively straight forward! Once you have read the workbook please take the time to visit my website www.how2become.com where you will find lots of information and advice on how to pass any job/career selection process.

MY BACKGROUND

I can remember sitting in the Armed Forces careers office in Preston, Lancashire at the age of 16 waiting patiently to see the Warrant Officer who would interview me as part of my application for joining the Royal Navy. I had already passed the written tests, and despite never having sat an interview before in my life, I was confident of success.

In the build-up to the interview I had worked very hard studying the job that I was applying for, and also working hard on my interview technique. At the end of the interview I was told that I had easily passed and all that was left to complete was the medical. Unfortunately I was overweight at the time and I was worried that I might fail. At the medical my fears became a reality and I was told by the doctor that I would have to lose a stone in weight before they would accept me. I walked out of the doctor's surgery and began to walk to the bus stop that would take me back home three miles away. I was absolutely gutted, and embarrassed, that I had failed at the final hurdle, all because I was overweight!

I sat at the bus stop feeling sorry for myself and wondering what job I was going to apply for next. My dream of joining the Armed Forces was over and I didn't know which way to turn. Suddenly, I began to feel a sense of determination to lose the weight and get fit in the shortest time possible. It was at that particular point in my life when things would change forever. As the bus approached I remember thinking there was no time like the present for getting started on my fitness regime. I therefore opted to walk the three miles home instead of being lazy and getting the bus. When I got home I sat in my room and wrote out a 'plan of action' that would dictate how I was going to lose the weight required. That plan of action was very simple and it said the following three things:

1. Every weekday morning I will get up at 6am and run 3 miles.

2. Instead of catching the bus to college and then back home again I will walk.

3. I will eat healthily and I will not go over the recommended daily calorific intake.

Every day I would read my simple 'action plan' and it acted as a reminder of what I needed to do. Within a few weeks of following my plan rigidly I had lost over a stone in weight and I was a lot fitter too!

When I returned back to the doctor's surgery for my medical the doctor was amazed that I had managed to lose the weight in such a short space of time and he was pleased that I had been so determined to pass the medical. Six months later I started my basic training course with the Royal Navy.

Ever since then I have always made sure that I prepare properly for any job application, interview or CV. If I do fail a particular application, interview or CV then I will always go out of my way to ask for feedback so that I can improve for next time.

Throughout my career I have always been successful. It's not because I am better than the next person, but simply because I prepare better. I didn't do very well at school so I have to work a lot harder to pass the exams and written tests that form part of a job application process but I am always aware of what I need to do and what I must improve on.

I have always been a great believer in preparation. Preparation was my key to success, and it also yours. Without the right level of preparation you will be setting out on the route to failure. Getting past the initial stages of a job selection process is tough, but if you follow the steps that I have compiled within this guide and use them as part of your preparation then you will increase your chances of success dramatically.

I want to stress from the offset that the vast majority of people who submit a CV do not get invited to interview and there are a couple of reasons for this failure– the CV they submit is usually out-of-date and it has very little relevance to the job they have applied for. If you want to be successful then your CV needs to be built around the job you are applying for, not built around yourself!

EMAIL ADDRESSES AND ANSWERPHONES

In addition to the above reasons for failure many job-seekers fail to think of the finer details when creating or submitting a CV. We now live in a digital world where social media and email are very much the norm; however, with these electronic formats and mediums comes a warning – your email address and Facebook account can tell a lot about you as a person. I have seen some very bizarre email addresses when inviting CV's to be submitted for a job that I have advertised. Why anyone would want to submit a CV via a personal email address that has some reference to the person's sexual desires is beyond me! You would be surprised at how often this happens- raunchysarah@.... was just one example. Call me judgemental, but I don't think it sets a very good impression of the person who has just applied for my office manager's post!

The point I am trying to make here is that you should be aware of things like this. If you leave a mobile telephone number contact on your CV make sure your answerphone message is appropriate and professional.

SOCIAL NETWORK SITES

Social network sites such as Facebook and Myspace can hinder and even stop your application process. Now please don't panic, I am not for one minute inferring that employers will check your Facebook or social media account before they invite you to interview, but is possible for them to do so.

You may or may not be aware but it is possible to search for someone on Facebook by simply typing their email address into the search bar on Facebook. If your account is 'unlocked' and set in 'public' mode then anyone can view your page. The point I am making here is that you should think carefully about the information that is on your Facebook and social media page(s). Let's assume that you are looking for a new job because you hate your boss. You have posted many comments on your Facebook profile expressing your disaffection for your job and your boss and your Facebook profile is public! How would it look to a potential employer? My advice is to make sure your social media sites are locked and not accessible to anyone other than your friends.

To further assist you in writing an effective CV I have created for you a free online training video and CV templates. You can watch the video and gain access to the CV templates at the following website:

www.CVwritingSkills.co.uk

Good luck and kind regards,

Richard McMunn

How2Become.com

CHAPTER 1
HOW TO
WRITE A CV

WHAT IS A CV?

The word Curriculum Vitae translated means the 'course of life'. CV's are used to demonstrate to an employer that you have the potential, the skills and the experience to carry out the role you are applying for. Your CV is a very important document and you should spend sufficient time designing it so that it matches the job that you are applying as closely as possible.

Why do people fail to get shortlisted?

The submission of a CV is usually the initial stage of any selection process. Most employers will place a job advert either in a newspaper or online with brief details of the job attached inviting people to apply for the post by way of submitting their CV. The vast majority of people will send off their 'generic' CV by email and then wonder why they never receive a reply.

I have heard many people complain that they never hear back from a potential employer, despite submitting what they believe to be a fantastic CV and covering letter. Whilst I agree it is rude for an employer not to respond to every CV that they receive, I can understand why they don't. I have been fortunate enough to work in both the public and private sectors. In the public sector we always acknowledged every CV that was submitted and I genuinely believe this was good practice. However, in the public sector most managers do not understand how a business runs, nor do they understand how valuable time is as a resource. When you own a business you have to make sure that every minute of your working day is used to promote growth and profitability for your company; sending out acknowledgment emails and letters to submitted CV's does not fall into either of these categories!

So, as a job applicant you have to understand how your average business owner or head of department operates – in a nutshell, they are very busy people and as such you need to make your CV as appealing and as effective as possible. If you do this, then they will notice your CV and you will get shortlisted; it's as simple as that!

What makes an effective CV?

In simple terms, an effective CV is one that matches the person specification and the requirements of the job you are applying for. Your CV should be used as a tool to assist you during the selection process and it should be centred on the following areas:

- Creating the right impression of yourself;
- Indicating that you possess the right qualities and attributes to perform the role of the job you are applying for;
- Grabbing the assessor's attention;
- Being concise, succinct and clear;
- Providing evidence of your relevant skills and qualifications.

The most effective CV's are the ones that make the assessor's job easy. They are simple to read, to the point, relevant and they also focus on the job/role that you are applying for. CV's should not be overly long unless an employer specifically asks for this. Effective CV writing is an acquired skill that can be obtained relatively quickly with a little bit of time, effort and focus.

Most people are guilty of creating one CV and submitting it for many different jobs; this is a big mistake. Although it involves additional work, your CV should be tweaked, amended and updated for EVERY job you apply for.

Before you begin to start work on your CV it is a good idea to have a basic idea of how a job/person specification is constructed. A job description/ person specification is basically a blueprint for the role you are applying for; it sets out what the employer expects from potential applicants. One of your main focus points during the construction of your CV will be to match the job/person specification using keywords and phrases. Most job/person specifications will include the following areas:

EXPERIENCE REQUIRED: previous jobs, unpaid work experience, life experience, skills, knowledge and abilities: for example, languages, driving, knowledge of specialist fields, ability to use equipment, plus some indication of the level of competence required, and whether the person must have the skills or knowledge beforehand or can learn them on the job.

QUALIFICATIONS REQUIRED: exams, certificates, degrees, diplomas (some jobs require specific qualifications, but most do not and it can be fairer to ask for the skills or knowledge represented by the qualification rather than asking for the qualification itself).

PERSONAL ATTRIBUTES REQUIRED: such as strength, ability to lift, willingness to work in a hectic busy environment or on one's own.

PERSONAL CIRCUMSTANCES: such as being able to work weekends or evenings or even to travel.

Most job/person specifications will be based around a task analysis of the vacancy, so there should be nothing within the job description/person specification that is irrelevant or that does not concern the particular role you are applying for. Whatever requirements you are asked to meet, you should try hard to match them as closely as possible, providing evidence if possible of your previous experience.

Matching the job description
This short section is very important, so please read it carefully and try to understand how to match the job description when creating your CV.

As already stated a job description is the blueprint for the role you're applying for. Whenever I advertise a job vacancy with my company I will sit down and think about the skills, qualities and attributes that I want the successful candidate to possess. Once I know what these are I will write the job description and person specification.

Here is a sample person specification and job description for a retail customer services assistant:

Retail Customer Service Assistant

JOB DESCRIPTION AND PERSON SPECIFICATION

We are looking for someone who is:

- Passionate about retail.
- Focusing on the customer and striving to understand them better than anyone.
- Driven to achieve results through determination and commitment.
- Committed to treating people in a fair and consistent way.
- Willing to roll their sleeves up to get things done.
- Determined to respond energetically to customer feedback.
- Motivated to work in partnership with others to achieve individual and team objectives.
- Adaptable and flexible to thrive in a 24/7 business.
- Devoted to seeking feedback on their performance and investing time in their own development.

Within your job you will need to perform the following tasks:

- Maintain excellent store standards
- Achieve customer service target levels
- Deal with customers in a friendly and positive manner
- Ensure compliance with food safety standards
- Deal with disputes and customer complaints in a constructive and positive way.
- Detect and prevent shop lifters
- Carry out duties of a checkout assistant where applicable
- Issue exchange and refunds brought to the CS desk.

The first step in creating an effective CV is to obtain a copy of the person specification and the job description. You then need to highlight the key skills, qualities and attributes within the document(s) and write them down on a separate piece of paper or word document. In order to demonstrate how this is achieve I will provide you with the same retail customer service assistant job description/person specification with the keywords/areas highlighted.

Retail Customer Service Assistant

JOB DESCRIPTION AND PERSON SPECIFICATION

We are looking for someone who is:

- <u>Passionate</u> about retail.
- <u>Focusing on the customer</u> and striving to understand them better than anyone.
- Driven to <u>achieve results</u> through determination and commitment.
- Committed to <u>treating people in a fair</u> and consistent way.
- Willing to roll their sleeves up to <u>get things done</u>.
- <u>Determined</u> to respond energetically to customer feedback.
- Motivated to <u>work in partnership</u> with others to achieve individual and team objectives.
- Adaptable and <u>flexible</u> to thrive in a 24/7 business.
- Devoted to <u>seeking feedback</u> on their performance and investing time in their own development.

Within your job you will need to perform the following tasks:

- Maintain <u>excellent store standards</u>
- <u>Achieve</u> customer service <u>target levels</u>
- <u>Deal with customers</u> in a friendly and positive manner
- Ensure <u>compliance</u> with food safety standards
- <u>Deal with disputes</u> and customer complaints in a constructive and positive way.
- Detect and <u>prevent shop lifters</u>
- Carry out <u>duties of a checkout assistant</u> where applicable
- <u>Issue exchange and refunds</u> brought to the CS desk.

Once we have worked through the document and highlighted the key areas, skills and requirements we now have something to work with. Here's the list of key requirements for the post:

• Passionate;

• Customer focused;

• An ability to achieve;

• Treating others fairly;

• Being motivated to get things done;

• Determined;

• Being able to listen to customers feedback;

• An ability to work with others as part of a team both internally and externally;

• A flexible approach to work;

• An ability to continually improve;

• Continuous professional development;

• Excellent standards;

• Able to achieve target levels and goals;

• Able to follow rules and apply set standards.

• Deal with customer complaints;

• Awareness;

• An ability to work on a checkout;

• Able to issue exchanges and refunds.

Once you have created your list detailing the requirements, skills and attributes for the job you are now able to start creating you CV and building it around the list you have compiled. By following the above process for every job you apply for you will be greatly increasing your chances of success.

Every great CV will contain a personal statement which describes your own personal qualities and the reasons why you have applied for the job. It doesn't have to be a long statement, but sufficient enough to tell the reader that you are the person they need to interview. If I was applying for the above retail customer services assistant job then my personal statement would look like this:

SAMPLE PERSONAL STATEMENT

"I am a highly passionate and determined person who can be totally relied upon to carry out a competent and professional job. I have extensive experience of working in a customer-focused environment and always put the customer first. I understand that the customer is crucial to an organisations success and can be relied upon to deal with customer complaints effectively whilst listening to their concerns and feedback. I am an excellent team player who genuinely believes in the importance of treating others fairly and diligently. I maintain excellent standards and always look for ways to improve my personal and professional development by seeking feedback from my managers. Finally, I am a dedicated and flexible person who I believe would be a valuable asset to your team and organisation."

You will see that the above statement is both powerful, hard-hitting and focused on matching the requirements of the role. Once again, I will highlight the keywords and phrases that are relevant to the key requirements of the post:

HOW THE PERSONAL STATEMENT MATCHES THE REQUIREMENTS OF THE JOB

*"I am a highly **passionate** and **determined** person who can be totally relied upon to carry out a competent and professional job. I have extensive experience of working in a **customer-focused environment** and always **put the customer first**. I understand that the customer is crucial to an organisations success and can be relied upon to deal with **customer complaints effectively** whilst **listening to their concerns and feedback**. I am an **excellent team player** who genuinely believes in the importance of **treating others fairly** and diligently. I maintain **excellent standards** and always look for ways to **improve my personal and professional development** by **seeking feedback** from my managers. Finally, I am a dedicated and **flexible person** who I believe would be a valuable asset to your team and organisation."*

I fully appreciate that following the above method and practices takes time; however, I hope you can see how effective it is at helping you to create a CV that matches the requirements of the job. I can guarantee that the underlined keywords and phrases will catch the attention of the person reading/assessing your CV and your chances of being shortlisted will increase greatly.

Of course, the personal statement is only a small element of your CV and you will have further opportunities to demonstrate your worth within the other areas of the CV. Before I go in to more detail about how you can create an awesome CV, let us first of all take a look at what the person assessing your CV is looking for.

WHAT IS THE PERSON ASSESSING YOUR CV LOOKING FOR?

As previously stated you should ensure that you make the assessor's job as simple as possible. Try to put yourself in the shoes of the assessor. How would you want an applicant's CV to look? You would want it to be relevant to role they are applying for and you would want it to be neat, concise and well organised.

For the majority of jobs out there, there will be a job specification and/or person specification. You need to spend some time thinking about the type of person they are looking for and how you can match the specification that is relevant to the job you want as already covered. Most job specifications will list the essential/desirable requirements in terms of education, qualifications, training, experience, skills, personality and any other special requirements.

Let's now take a look at another job description and person specification for an entirely different job. The job description and person specification that follows is for the role of a Physical Training Instructor with a local gymnasium.

QUALIFICATIONS REQUIRED	ABOUT THE JOB
You will need 2 GCSEs/SCEs or equivalent, in the subjects of English language at Grade C/3 minimum and in Mathematics at Grade G/6 minimum. You will need to have a good standard of fitness in a number of sports and have the ability to swim. You will be assessed via a specialist interview and be required to undertake additional tests.	Physical Training Instructors are responsible for organising and arranging physical fitness training programmes for all members of our gymnasium. Therefore, a good standard of physical fitness and organisational skills are required. In addition to being physically fit you must also possess good motivational skills and be capable of: • Managing and arranging adventure activities; • Managing sporting facilities; • Organising and conducting instructional classes; • Performing fitness tests; • Arranging and holding sports counselling sessions.

You will see from the above details that some of the key elements of the role include suitable levels of physical fitness, good organisational skills, motivational skills and the ability to manage people and resources. Once you have the above information then you will be able to mold your CV around the key aspects of the job.

Before I provide you with a sample CV that is based on matching the above role, let's first of all take a look at some of the key elements of a CV.

THE KEY ELEMENTS OF A CV

The following is a list of information I recommend you include within your CV. Try to put them in this order and remember to be brief and to the point. Make sure you include and highlight the positive aspects of your experience and achievements.

- YOUR PERSONAL DETAILS
- YOUR PERSONAL STATEMENT
- YOUR EMPLOYMENT HISTORY
- YOUR ACADEMIC ACIEVEMENTS
- YOUR INTERESTS
- ANY OTHER INFORMATION
- YOUR REFERENCES

Let's now take a look at each of the above sections and what you need to include.

YOUR PERSONAL DETAILS

When completing this section you should include the following details:

- Your full name
- Address
- Date of birth
- Nationality
- Contact telephone numbers including home and mobile
- E mail address

YOUR PERSONAL STATEMENT

To begin with try to write a brief but to the point statement about yourself making sure you include the keywords that best describe your character. Some effective words to use when describing yourself might include:

Ambitious, enthusiastic, motivated, caring, trustworthy, meticulous, sense of humour, drive, character, determination, will to succeed, passionate, loyal, teamwork, hard working.

The above words are all powerful and positive aspects of an individual's character. Try to think of your own character and what positive words you can use that best describe you.

Within your profile description try to include a statement that is relative to you and that will make the assessor think you are the right person for the job. Although I have already provided you with one for a retail customer services assistant, here is one for the role of a physical training instructor:

"I am an extremely fit and active person who has a great deal of experience in this field and I have a track record of high achievement. I have very good organisational and motivational skills and I am always striving to improve myself. I believe that I would embrace the challenges that this new role has to offer."

YOUR EMPLOYMENT HISTORY

When completing this section try to ensure that it is completed in reverse chronological order. Provide the reader with dates, locations and employers and remember to include your job title. Give a brief description of your main achievements and try once again to include words of a positive nature, such as:

- *Achieved*
- *Developed*
- *Progressed*
- *Managed*
- *Created*
- *Succeeded*
- *Devised*
- *Drove*
- *Expanded*
- *Directed*

It is also a good idea to quantify your main achievements, such as:

"During my time with this employer I was responsible for motivating my team and organising different activities."

YOUR ACADEMIC ACHIEVEMENTS

When completing this section include the dates, names and locations of the schools, colleges or universities that you attended in chronological order.

You should also include your qualifications and any other relevant achievements such as health and safety qualifications or first aid qualifications. Anything that is relevant to the role you're applying for would be an advantage.

YOUR INTERESTS

Within this section try to include interests that match the requirements of the job and ones that also portray you in a positive manner. Maybe you have worked within the voluntary sector or have even carried out some charity work in the past? If so, try to include these in your CV as they show you have a caring and concerning nature. You may also play sports or keep fit, in which case you should include these too. If you have any evidence of where you have worked effectively as part of a team then include these also. In order to assist you I will now provide you with some sample hobbies and pastimes and details of how they can improve your CV:

Reading – This demonstrates you are an intelligent individual who looks for ways to improve their knowledge of subjects. It also shows that you are capable of relaxing, which in turn improves health.

Visiting the gym and playing sports – These demonstrate you are a team player as well as having a desire to keep yourself fit. If you keep fit and healthy then you are less likely to take time off sick.

Playing a musical instrument – This demonstrates you have the patience and ability to learn something new. It also demonstrates you have the ability to concentrate for long periods of time.

Voluntary work – This shows you have a dedicated and caring nature. Putting voluntary work on your CV is very powerful!

Spending time with your family – This shows you are a stable and secure person.

ANY OTHER INFORMATION

Within this section of your CV you can include any other information that is relevant to your skills or experiences that you may feel are of benefit. Examples of these could include certificates of achievement from work or school.

REFERENCES

It is good practice to include two references at the end of your CV. Try to include your current or previous employer, providing you know that they are going to write positive things about you. Be careful who you choose as a reference and make sure you seek their permission first prior to putting down their name and contact details. It may also be a good idea to ask them if you can have a copy of what they have written about you for reference later.

SAMPLE CV

Let's now take a look at a sample CV to explain how it all fits together. The following sample CV has been designed to give you an idea of how an effective CV might look. It has been created with the position of Physical Training Instructor in mind. All of the information provided is fictitious. Although not essential to place it here, you will see that the personal statement has a far better impact if it is placed near the beginning of the CV.

Curriculum Vitae of Richard McMunn

Address: 75, Any Street, Anytown, Anyshire. ANY 123
Date of birth: 01/01/1970
Nationality: British
Telephone contact: 01227 XXXXX / Mobile 07890 XXX XXX
E Mail contact: richardmcmunn@anyemailaddress.co.uk

Personal profile of Richard McMunn

I am an extremely fit and active person who has a great deal of experience in this field and I have a track record of high achievement. I have very good organisational and motivational skills and I am always striving to improve myself. I believe that I would embrace the challenges that this new role has to offer. I am a motivated, dedicated, loyal and ambitious person who has the ability to work both within a team and also unsupervised.

I already have a large amount of experience in the working environment and take on a large number of responsibilities both at work, around the home and in my leisure time activities. I am currently the Captain of my local football team and part of my responsibilities includes organising and conducting weekly evening training sessions for the team. For every training session that I run I always try to vary the type of exercises that we perform. This allows me to maintain everyone's motivation and interest levels. For example, one week I will organise the Multi Stage Fitness Test and another week we will practice tackling and dribbling skills.

To conclude, I am a fit, motivated active, organised and professional individual who has a lot of skills and experiences to offer your organisation.

Employment history of Richard McMunn
(in chronological order)

Job position/title/company #1 goes here   Date of employment goes here
During my time with this employer I was responsible for motivating my team and organising different activities.

Job position/title/company #2 goes here   Date of employment goes here
During my time with this employer I was responsible stock taking and dealing with customer's queries and complaints. I also took on the responsibility of arranging the company's annual staff leisure activity event which often included some form of motivational talk.

Job position/title/company #3 goes here   Date of employment goes here
During my time with this employer I undertook a training course in health and safety and first aid. Part of my role included managing resources and training rooms/equipment.

Academic achievements of Richard McMunn

Health and Safety qualification	Date of achievement goes here
First Aid qualification	Date of achievement goes here
Level 1 Physical Training Instructor qualification	Date of achievement goes here
GSCE Maths Grade C	Date of achievement goes here
GCSE English Grade C	Date of achievement goes here
GCSE Physical Education Grade B	Date of achievement goes here

Interests and Hobbies of Richard McMunn
I am an extremely fit and active person who carries out a structured training programme at my local gym five times a week. During my training sessions I will carry out a variety of different exercises such as indoor rowing, cycling, treadmill work and light weights. I measure my fitness levels by performing

the multi-stage fitness test once a week and I can currently achieve level 14.5. In addition to my gym work I am a keen swimmer and break up my gym sessions with long swim sessions twice a week. I can swim 60 lengths of my local swimming pool in time of 35 minutes.

I am also the Captain of my local football team and play in the position of midfield. I am also responsible for organising and arranging the weekly training sessions.

In addition to my sporting activities I like to relax with a weekly Yoga group at my local community centre. I also have a keen interest in art and attend evening classes during the months October through to December.

Further information

Six months ago I decided to carry out a sponsored fitness event in order to raise money for a local charity. I swam 60 lengths of my local swimming pool, and then ran 26 miles before cycling 110 miles all in one day. In total I managed to raise over £10,000 for charity.

References

Name, address and contact details of reference #1

Name, address and contact details of reference #2

You see that the above CV is only 2.5 pages in length, yet it is relevant, concise and provides an excellent overview of the applicants' skills, qualities and attributes that relate to the post.

The key to success when creating a CV is to ensure the CV matches the job you are applying for. The vast majority of people submit a 'generic' CV that does not match the role they are applying and is not up-to-date.

If you put in a little bit of effort when completing your CV you will greatly increase your chances of success. Remember this rule:

NEW JOB APPLICATION = NEW CV!

In the next section of this workbook I will provide you with a number of sample CVs to help you gain a better understanding of what makes a great CV.

CHAPTER 2
CV SAMPLES

The following sample CV's use fictitious information, names and contact details. Any relevance to living persons or otherwise is coincidence. The CV's have been created to give you an idea of how some of the best CV's are constructed. There is not set format for constructing a CV and you will see that they all vary in content, design and presentation. Your CV should be unique to you! To help explain some of the more positive aspects of each CV I have indicated in boxes the pertinent information to explain why the CV is effective.

CV of Susan Gray

ADDRESS:
34 Fictown Street
Fictown
Fictshire
FC1TY6

Effective use of white space which makes the CV far easier to read. This CV is organised and professional looking.

TELEPHONE:
Telephone numbers go here.

EMAIL:
Email address goes here.

DATE OF BIRTH:
D.O.B. goes here.

MARITAL STATUS:
Married

NATIONALITY:
British

PERSONAL STATEMENT:
I am a hard-working, conscientious and dedicated person who has developed a trackrecord for delivering targets that are set by my superiors and can be relied upon to excel in any role given. I have a Diploma in management. Studies and a certificate in bookkeeping/accounts.

EDUCATIONAL QUALIFICATIONS:
Insert your qualifications and the year obtained here.

EMPLOYMENT HISTORY:
OFFICE MANAGER
Company name goes here

Feb 03 - Present

• Provided first line support and day to day administration for Operations Manager.

• Involved with day to day HR issues and administration.

• Coordinated projects on behalf of Operations Manager.

• Managed, supported and lead the administration and reception team.

• Managed all fleet vehicles on site, ensuring all documentation, maintenance and safety aspects were met.

• Liaised and worked closely with the clients Administration Manager to ensure we provided the best service possible.

Key achievements

· Enhanced the reception area and team which resulted in a more professional and guest-focused service.

· Streamlined and trained the reception team to enable them to carry out additional administration duties during quiet periods.

· Played an integral part in forming a strong management team. Working towards goals and through many changes within the company.

· I became a vital part of the organisations 'Crisis Management Team' which came with a different set of responsibilities.

The use of bullet points makes this CV easier to read. The key elements of the job are detailed.

CUSTOMER SERVICE ASSISTANT
Company name goes here

Nov 95 – Feb 03

· Provided support to staff and Directors in all aspects of administration.

· Managed, supported and lead the administration team to ensure service, productivity and moral was high.

· Managed and worked with IT.

· Supported and managed the administration of three regional offices.

· Responsible for complete facilities management and Health and Safety.

· Provided strategies and generated ideas according to business needs.

· Managed HR policies and recruitment.

This CV makes effective use of bold headlines and titles which make the CV look organised and professional.

Key achievements:

· Entered into a company with difficulties in service, organisation and staffing issues. Implemented a structured, team orientated and customer-focused environment.

· Initiated and successfully obtained Investors in People.

• Provided and initiated many ideas which gave the company a more professional approach to both external clients and staff.

• Initiated a PO system to enable accountability and traceability.

FURTHER ACADEMIC
ACHIEVEMENTS
AND INTERESTS

Pitman general:
Certificate in bookkeeping and accounts / typing skills (50wpm) / Diploma in management studies.

Travel and Tourism:
COTAC Air Travel and Package Tours papers 1&2.

REFERENCES: Provide names, addresses, and contacts here.

This is a powerful personal statement. This individual has limited work experience and therefore needs to provide a strong opening statement.

Marcus Grainger CV

34 Fictown Street, Fictown, Fictshire. FT11TW

Date of Birth: Insert here   **Email:** Insert here   **Mobile:** Insert here

Personal statement

I am a highly organised and conscientious team player who has a great passion for sports and fitness. My strengths lie in my ability to organise teams and achieve targets and I always take up the opportunity to learn new and interesting skills. More recently I achieved grade 5 in guitar which I believe demonstrates my ability to learn and retain information. I strongly feel that my skills and achievements to date would be of benefit to your organisation and would thrive in a working environment that prides itself on professionalism.

Academic

2008- 2011: Smithtown University
Events management, BA (HONS) 2:2

Modules studied included: Project Management, Tourism Development, Marketing, French and German.

These are excellent additional qualifications to include in your CV.

2005- 2008: Fictown Grammar School
4 A-Levels (A-E grades): PE, Biology, ICT & Design Technology.

Achievements & Certificates

Work experience training: Manual Handling, Health & Safety, Risk Assessment, First Aid and Fire Awareness.

During my time at university I became involved with the sports society as their president for two years representing the Students' Union and University whilst organising trips to France for large groups of students. I also volunteered as a team leader during Fresher's Week and helped to plan and co-ordinate large events with the Students' Union including their annual Summer ball.

Volunteer Employment

- Artist Liaison for Fictown Student Union events (3 years).

- Boardmasters Steward.

- Entertainment Officer for Fictown Student Union (1 year) – running of the Summer Ball and Student Union events on a weekly basis.

- Events Crew Member of Fictown Student Union (2 years) – total of over 250 hours.

- Spent eight weeks working at a local charity shop to gain work experience skills.

Employment History

Sept 2011 – Present   Fictown holiday resorts agency

Sales co-ordinator whose main responsibilities include sale of catered and self-catered properties including resort transfers, updating availability on daily basis and dealing with clients and agents via emails and over the phone.

This individual has limited work experience. However, they have carried out lots of voluntary work which is good!

Summer Break representative 2011

Working as a Summer Break representative which involved ensuring the satisfaction of the clients at summer break as well as organising coach arrivals and departures and administering first aid when required.

Personal Interests

My favourite sport is rugby which I have a great passion for and wish to take further participation within in the future. I enjoy attending music festivals as I am a keen guitarist who has achieved grade 5 level through continued tuition. I try to travel as much as I can as I love to experience new things and widen my horizons. I apply to volunteering positions as much as possible as I enjoy working at events regardless of being paid as I feel that the experience is so much more appealing as well as the interaction I get with a multitude of different people.

Skills

- Competent in the use of Microsoft Word, Excel and PowerPoint to A-Level standard and also have a basic understanding of Access and Dreamweaver.

- Work well as a team player and as an individual. I am hardworking, keen to learn new skills and highly organised in every aspect of my life.

- I have over 5 years' experience of customer relations and sales with my extensive background in both bar work, sales and representative work.

- Full and clean driving licence.

- Providing excellent customer service: customer focused employment.

- Excellent project management skills with a proven track record for delivering set targets and deadlines.

- Level grade 5 guitar.

References

Insert the names and contact details of two references here.

MARIA DOHERTY

Fictown, Fictshire
Email address goes here
Telephone number goes here

> This CV follows a slightly different format; however, it is full of work-related skills and qualifications that will appeal to any employer.

PROFILE

A highly motivated Administrator with over 20 years' experience in all areas from reception to office management, most recently managing the day to day operational aspects of a Business Centre, including accounts, tenancy agreements and health and safety.

Able to provide exceptional first line contact, both face-to-face and via the telephone with various department, tenants, maintenance personnel, sub-contractors and general public. Outstanding team player developed through my career working alongside colleagues at all levels but also with the ability to use own initiative; thriving on undertaking individual responsibilities.

Overall, taking pride in everything that I set out to achieve, ensuring that it is completed to a high personal standard and within given timeframes.

KEY SKILLS

- Proficient in MS Office (Word, Excel, Outlook and Access), internet, emails and technology advances.

- Ability to remain calm and diplomatic at all times in a pressurised environment.

- Excellent communication skills both written and verbal.

- Methodical and organised.

- Willingness to train and learn new skills.

- Accurate data entry with an eye for detail.

- Ability to prioritise workloads and multi task to always meet deadlines.

- Diary and social event management.

- Knowledge of Sage, Focus and various switchboard systems.

- Website maintenance.

CAREER SUMMARY

November 2008 – June 2011 Business Centre Manager

- Ensuring the smooth running of a Business Centre.

- Front line management.

- Negotiating with tenants.

- Composing licence agreements.

- Taking monthly rental payments and chasing arrears.

- Achieving and maintaining approximately 95% occupancy.

- Liaising with maintenance personnel and subcontractors.

- Arranging charity and networking events.

- Meeting room management, including catering.

- Health and safety, including weekly fire drill.

- Maintaining company website.

- Parking control.

July 2004 – November 2008 Senior Administrator

- Providing assistance to the Office Manager.

- Providing support to the Agency and Professional teams working with a Commercial Property Sales and Lettings environment.

- Front line support, being the first point of contact for visitors and callers.

- Preparing files for bank instructions with competitor analysis and building reports.

- Arranging Surveyor viewings and valuation appointments.

- Maintaining client databases.

- Preparing marketing particulars and uploading to company website.

- Distributing incoming post and preparing outgoing mail.

- Mail shots.

- Maintaining an inventory of building keys.

- Creating an archive filing system.

- Stationery ordering and negotiating deals with suppliers.

July 2001 – August 2003 Senior Administrator/Assistant to Sales & Office Manager

- Providing Support to the Advertising Sales Manager and Office Manager.

- Assisting the Project Manager at annual awards events.

- Providing software support to colleagues alongside the IT Department.

- Account management.

- Order processing within an advertising sales environment.

- Liaising with customers.

- Maintaining client databases and sales spread sheets.

- General office duties.

EDUCATION & TRAINING

- Fictown Comprehensive School, Fictown.

- 4 GCSE's in English, Maths, Business Studies and Information Studies.

- Pitman's Typing and Word-processing.

- NVQ Level II Business Administration.

- Competent in IT with an advanced knowledge of the Microsoft Office package.
  I also keep abreast of the current social networking and technology advances.
  I am currently embarked on a refresher course in Sage Line 50.

INTERESTS & HOBBIES

I enjoy music, singing, cooking, films, swimming, country walks, photography, sport and socialising. I have a good sense of humour and enjoy making new friends and acquaintances. I am currently training for a sponsored swim and will raise £2000 for a local charity.

I am a volunteer for Scope, helping people with disabilities get into work.

I hold a full, clean driving licence.

References available on request

If you are unsure who to nominate as a reference it is acceptable to put this. However, I would recommend you include actual reference details whenever possible.

JENNY BROUGHTON

55 – Smithtown Street – Smithtown – Smithshire – SM1SHT
Phone: 0789018XXX · Email JennyBroughton@...

This CV uses Times New Roman font. It looks concise and professional.

PERSONAL PROFILE

I am an enthusiastic, hardworking and reliable person who has gained invaluable experience in the customer-care industry. I have a positive and caring nature and believe I can bring a number of excellent skills and attributes to your organisation.

SKILLS AND ACHIEVEMENTS

COMPUTER LITERACY

- Extensive experience with the Microsoft Office software suite and similar programs in both the academic and work environment.

- Successfully used HTML and professional software packages to design and upgrade websites. Proficient in the use of Dreamweaver and Wordpress.

- Proven ability to utilise online database sources effectively for academic based research.

- Confident typing ability at 65 words per minute.

CUSTOMER SERVICE EXPERIENCE

- Customer service awareness and skills developed through working in service environments requiring face to face, telephone and written communication with customers.

- Experience of working with customers in a one to one environment providing service where needed.

- Strong ability to interact in a persuasive and confident manner with customers.

- Proven ability to think quickly on my feet and respond to complicated questioning in a pressured environment.

Effective use of bullet points to emphasis key skills.

EFFECTIVE COMMUNICATION

• Held the position of head of the Student Union at university which required effective communication with students and agents both internal and external to the university.

• Well-developed oral presentation skills as a result of competing in a pressurised environment.

• Travelling to many places around the world has developed my ability to communicate effectively with people from different social and cultural backgrounds.

INITIATIVE AND MOTIVATION

• Introduced the annual charity event at university which raises money for local charities through sponsored events.

• Arranging events such as the London to Brighton cycle ride which we raised over £5000 for local good causes.

TEAMWORK AND LEADERSHIP

• Strong teamwork skills due to experience working with a variety of different people in a wide range of environments, ranging from office and sales environments to being head of the Student Union at university

EDUCATION

Smithtown College

A-Level: Law (A2 grade B, AS grade B), Government and Politics (A2 grade B, AS grade B) and Geography (A2 grade C, AS grade B)

Smithtown Senior School

GCSE: English Literature, A; English Language, B; Mathematics, B; Biology, B; Physics, B; Art, B; Chemistry, B; French, B; Geography, C

WORK EXPERIENCE

2005–2006   **Sales Assistant**
Smithtown charity shop

Summer of 2007   **Post office**
General administration work

2008 – Jan 2011   **Customer care department**
Looking after the organisations previous customers.

REFERENCES

Employers' reference: Michael Jameson – 0789018XXX

Personal reference: Julia Bishop – 0789018XXX

This CV is not a traditional layout; however, it is highly effective at indicating the individual's personal qualities and attributes that would be suitable to the post. By listing the different key elements such as 'customer service experience' and 'work experience she is making it clear that she has the relevant skills for the post being applied for.

CURRICULUM VITAE

SURNAME: Marsham

FORENAMES: Rebecca Katie

DATE OF BIRTH: 11th of September 1987

ADDRESS: 54, Smithtown street
                      Smithtown
                      Smithshire
                      SM14TY

TELEPHONE NO.:   07890183XXX

EMAIL: rebeccamarsham@emailadresshere.co.uk

Although this person lacks experience their CV is well-structured, easy to read and makes good use of their skills and attributes acquired to date.

PERSONAL PROFILE

I currently have a weekend job as an assistant in a café and I have previously worked as an assistant in a fish and chip shop. I enjoy working and dealing with customers and I can provide excellent customer service. I am very hard working, trustworthy and I look forward to new challenges. I have also gained valuable office work experience carrying out voluntary work for my local Parish Council. During my time there I gained experience in answering the phones, photocopying, inputting data, dealing with booking enquiries and generally helping out where needed. I also have experience in using Microsoft Word, PowerPoint, Excel and Outlook.

EDUCATION

Smithtown School, Smithtown Road, Smithstreet.
(April 2008 – June 2011)

GCSES	GRADE
English Literature	A
English Language	C
Maths	C
Business Studies	B
ICT	B
Additional Science	B
Core Science	C
Child Development	E

This is a good personal profile which would suit an application for a job in customer care, voluntary work or administration.

Level 2 BTEC Diploma

Performing Arts 4x Distinction = 4 x A* - JSLA Award*

EMPLOYMENT HISTORY

August 2011 – present	**Smithtown Café** London Road Smithtown SM15TY6

Position: **Weekend Assistant**

Main duties include taking orders from customers, handling cash, cleaning tables and assisting with duties in the kitchen.

April 2011 – July 2011	**Smithtown Fisheries** Fishy Road Smithtown SM14TY3

Position: **Part-time Assistant in fish and chip shop**

My main duties were taking orders, handling cash, ordering stock and serving customers with fish and chips.

HOBBIES AND INTERESTS

I enjoy walking and looking after my dogs, reading, listening to music, keeping fit, films and socialising with my friends

These are good hobbies and interests to include.

REFEREES

CURRENT EMPLOYER:	Mr R Roberts Smithtown Café London Road, Smithtown SM15TY6
FORMER EMPLOYER:	Mr A Marshall Fishy Road Smithtown SM14TY3
VOLUNTARY WORK SUPERVISOR:	Mrs M Bishops Community Centre Administrator, Smithtwon Parish Council, Smithtown SM14TY3

CV – Angela Cartwright

Name: Angela Cartwright
Address: Address goes here

Mobile Phone: 07890183XXX
E-mail: angelacartwright@...

Profile:
A proficient, dynamic and highly motivated individual with a good demonstrated ability to learn quickly, adapt easily, work methodically and accurately whilst striving for quality in every task. An effective communicator with people at all levels, easily making strong working relationships. Excellent organisational skills developed in a variety of deadline orientated situations.

Summary:
Experienced in providing extensive secretarial and administrative support to company Directors and appropriate proactive and responsive advice on issues including; recruitment & selection, training & development and motivation & reward to both Managers and employees. Proven track record in the implementation of procedures and processes as and when required to ensure the smooth running of any busy office.

EMPLOYMENT HISTORY

Smith Holidays
Position:
Duration:

Travel/Holiday Company
HR &Office Manager (Standalone Position)
May 2012 – Present

Responsibilities:

• Oversee and manage the office to ensure staff adhered to office regulations and policies (i.e. lateness, dress code).

• Daily rota management across all departments using a computerised system.

• Responsible for the condition and upkeep of the office premises.

• Recruitment (including managing and allocating interns).

• Ordering all stationery and office equipment.

Achievements:	Identified cost savings by examining office equipment needs, negotiating with suppliers and providing cost efficient alternatives, saving the business 20% in running costs.

Updating company policies and procedures in line with current employment law, such as the company handbook and contracts. Recommending and implementing a new rota and pay scheme for homeworkers which potentially generates more sales and has improved staff morale.

Smiths Books	Book Retailer & Publisher
Position:	HR Assistant/PA
Duration:	Jan 2005 - November 2009

Responsibilities:

- Administrative support to three HR Managers

- Extensive diary management and secretarial support to the HR and Training Director

- Creating and analysing quarterly absence and labour reports

- Administration for all new starters and leavers

- Preparing contracts

- Writing job descriptions

- Working closely with recruitment consultants from our PSL

- Assisting in first stage Interviews

- Organising and conducting Induction tours

Achievements:

Helped design and revise the company's staff handbook and completely revamped the various employment procedures.

Other achievements include mastering Excel and PeopleSoft so I was able to create and produce accurate reports as and when required and the Introduction of a Long Service Reward and Recognition scheme. Negotiating the best rates I organised the staff Christmas party for Head Office, (80 staff) on two occasions.

EDUCATION & TRAINING

Higher:	• 3 'A' Levels, Maths (B), English (A), History (B)
Certificates:	• HR Assistant
Basic:	• Passed all years at Spanish class
Safety:	• Health and safety awareness course

ADDITIONAL

Technology:	I have excellent knowledge of all Microsoft applications, the Internet and PeopleSoft.
Languages:	Excellent English, both written and spoken.
	Spanish at an intermediate level, spoken and written.
References:	Names of two references and contact details will go here.

CHAPTER 3
A STEP-BY-STEP GUIDE TO WRITING A CV

In this next section I want to provide you with a simple to follow, step-by-step guide to wring an effective CV. The steps that follow will incorporate all that I have explained so far within this guide. Let's get started:

STEP 1

The first stage is to identify which job you want to apply for. Most people will create a CV based around themselves before looking for a job to apply for. This is one of the main reasons for failure. In order to create an effective CV you first of all need to know what job you wish to get!

Most employers will advertise vacancies online, although some will still use local newspapers as a source to attract potential applicants.

STEP 2

Once you have identified the job/jobs that you want to apply for you should collect the person specification and job description for each post that you wish to apply for. This may simply mean copying the job description from the online advert.

Here is an example of a recent job advert that is in the customer service industry:

CUSTOMER SERVICE ASSISTANT/OPERATOR

GENERAL PURPOSE OF THE ROLE

Interact with customers to provide and process information in response to inquiries, concerns and requests about products and services.

Main Job Tasks and Responsibilities

- Deal directly with customers either by telephone, electronically or face-to-face.
- Respond promptly to customer inquiries.
- Handle and resolve customer complaints.
- Obtain and evaluate all relevant information to handle product and service inquiries.
- Provide pricing and delivery information.
- Process orders, forms, applications and requests.
- Record details of inquiries, comments and complaints.
- Maintain customer databases.
- Manage administration.

Education and Experience

- Minimum of 3 x GCSE's / O Levels grade C or above.
- Knowledge of customer service principles and practices.
- Knowledge of relevant computer applications.
- Ability to type.
- Knowledge of administrative procedures.

Key Competencies

- Interpersonal skills.
- Communication skills - verbal and written.
- Listening skills.

- Problem analysis and problem-solving.
- Attention to detail and accuracy.
- Customer service orientation.
- Adaptability.
- Initiative.
- Stress tolerance.

STEP 3

Once you have obtained a copy of the person specification/job description I recommend you use a highlighter pen to go through the documents and collate a list of the main skills and keywords/phrases that make up the CV. Whilst some of the attributes will be assessed at interview it is your job to provide as much evidence as possible within your CV to demonstrate you have the potential to carry out the job. If you do this, you will get an interview!

The following list of skills and keywords/phrases have been extracted from the above job description/person specification.

> Interact and deal with customers

> Respond to queries

> Resolve customer complaints

> Processing orders

> Maintain accurate records

> Maintain customer databases

> Good communication skills

> Problem solving abilities

> Attention to detail

> Adaptable

> Initiative

> Stress tolerance

STEP 4

Once you have created your list of skills and keywords/phrases taken from the person specification/job description you should then create your personal profile using as many of the keywords and phrases as possible. Here's an example of a personal profile based on the above list.

"I am a highly professional and adaptable person who has an excellent approach to work. Having worked in a customer focused environment I am able to interact and deal with customers in a highly proficient manner. I have extensive experience in dealing with customer complaints and pride myself on my excellent communication skills. I can work effectively in highly stressful environments and my attention to detail is excellent. Finally, I am competent at processing customer orders and maintaining customer databases."

You will notice that the above personal profile is deliberately suited to the job the person is applying for. When the assessor/employer reads this CV he or she will soon realise that this person has many of the key skills and attributes required for the job.

STEP 5

The final step is to incorporate the personal profile into you CV and also build your previous experiences and employment positions around the skills and experiences required for the post. You will see that the following simple CV does this effectively.

Although the CV is only two pages of A4 in length it is highly relevant to the post being advertised.

CURRICULUM VITAE

SURNAME:	McMunn
FORENAMES:	Richard Anthony
DATE OF BIRTH:	12th of August 1976
ADDRESS:	54, Smithtown Street
	Smithtown
	Smithshire
	SM14TY
TELEPHONE NO.:	07890183XXX
EMAIL:	richardmcmunn@emailadresshere.co.uk

PERSONAL PROFILE

I am a highly professional and adaptable person who has an excellent approach to work. Having worked in a customer focused environment I am able to interact and deal with customers in a highly proficient manner. I have extensive experience in dealing with customer complaints and pride myself on my excellent communication skills. I can work effectively in highly stressful environments and my attention to detail is excellent. Finally, I am competent at processing customer orders and maintaining customer databases.

EDUCATION

Smithtown School, Smithtown Road, Smithstreet.
(Dates go here)

GCSES	GRADE
English Literature	A
English Language	C
Maths	C
Business Studies	B
ICT	B
Additional Science	B
Core Science	C

Level 2 City and Guilds
Certificate in Customer Service

EMPLOYMENT HISTORY

August 2011 – present   **Smithtown Retail Shop**
London Road
Smithtown
SM15TY6

Position: **Customer services assistant**
Main duties include communicating with customers, taking orders from customers, dealing with queries and complaints and maintaining the customer database.

April 2011 – July 2011:   **Smithtown Warehouse Wholesalers**
Smith Road
Smithtown
SM14TY3

Position: **Customer services manager**

My main duties were dealing with customers on a daily basis, welcoming customers in to the shop and typing up customer promotional letters and order receipts.

HOBBIES AND INTERESTS

I enjoy walking and looking after my dogs, reading, listening to music, keeping fit, films and socialising with my friends.

REFEREES

CURRENT EMPLOYER   **Mr R Reynolds**
                              Smithtown Retail Shop
                              London Road
                              Smithtown
                              SM15TY6

PREVIOUS EMPLOYER   Susan Chambers
                              Smithtown Warehouse Wholesalers
                              Smith Road
                              Smithtown
                              SM14TY3

STEP 6

Once you have completed your CV make sure you check it for errors. There is nothing worse than receiving a CV from a job applicant which is strewn with spelling mistakes. In order to achieve this it may be worth while giving your CV to a friend or relative so they can give it a good check over for you. If you do this, make sure the person helping you out can spell themselves!

STEP 7

The final step is to send off your CV with a covering letter or note. The vast majority of CV's are now submitted online or via email. Here is an example of a good covering note to send with a CV that is submitted by email:

Name: Richard McMunn
Email address: richardmcmunn@emailaddresshere.co.uk

SUBJECT: Application for Customer Services Assistant

Dear sir/madam,

Please find attached my CV in support of my application for the position of Customer Service Assistant with your company. I believe that I possess the skills, qualities and attributes required to perform the role to an exceptional standard and feel strongly that I would be a great asset to your company.

I would very much like the opportunity to prove my skills to you at interview and can be contacted on 07890183XXX at any time.

Yours faithfully,
Richard McMunn

You will note that in the covering letter I have included a contact telephone number. Whilst not essential this demonstrates my level of keenness to be invited to interview.

When signing off a letter or email then follow this rule for the use of 'sincerely' and 'faithfully':

If you know their name, use sincerely. If you don't know their name, use faithfully.

Dear Mr Smith = Yours sincerely

Dear Sir = Yours faithfully

CHAPTER 4
FURTHER TIPS FOR CREATING YOUR CV

New application = new CV

It is important that every time you apply for a job you re-evaluate the content of your CV so that you can match the skills and qualifications required. As a rule you should complete a new CV for every job application, unless your applications are close together and the job/person specification is relatively the same. Don't become complacent or allow your CV to get out-of-date.

The main reason why most people do not get invited to interview is simply because their CV does not match the skills, qualities and experiences required to perform the advertised role. As mentioned previously, you must get in to the habit of structuring your CV around the person specification for the job you are applying for. If you take the time to follow this advice then I guarantee you will soon see your luck start to change when you apply for jobs.

Don't pad out your CV

There is a common misconception amongst many job applicants that you need to make your CV scores of pages long for it to get recognised. This simply isn't true. When creating your CV aim for quality rather than quantity. If I was looking through an applicant's CV then I would much prefer to see three pages of high quality focused information rather than 30 pages padded out with irrelevance.

Create a positive image

Writing an effective CV involves a number of important aspects. One of those is the manner in which you present your CV. When developing your CV ask yourself the following questions:

- Is my spelling, grammar and punctuation correct?
- Is my CV legible and easy to read?
- Is the style in which I am writing my CV standardised?
- Is my CV neat and does it look presentable?
- Is the CV constructed in a logical manner?

By following the above tips in respect of your CV image you will be on the right track to improving your chances of getting the job you are after. You should spend just as much time on the **presentation** of your CV as you do on the **content**.

Finally, in relation to CV presentation, do not use overly-stylish fonts that look good, yet can be difficult to read. Think about the person assessing your CV; they do not have a lot of time to spend reading every CV that is presented in front of them so go out of your way to make their life easier.

Do you have the right qualities and attributes for the job you are applying for?

When you are developing your CV have a look at the required personal qualities that are listed within the job/person spec. Try to match these as closely as possible but, again, ensure that you provide examples where appropriate. For example, in the sample job description for a Physical Training Instructor one of the required personal qualities was to:

'Organise and conduct instructional classes'

Try and provide an example of where you have achieved this in any previous roles. The following is a fictitious example of how this might be achieved:

"I am currently the Captain of my local football team and part of my *responsibilities include **organising** and **conducting** weekly evening training sessions for the team. For every training session that I run I always try to vary the type of exercises that we perform. This allows me to maintain everyone's motivation and interest levels. For example, one week I will organise the Multi Stage Fitness Test for them and another week I will arrange practice tackling and dribbling skills."*

Matching your qualities and attributes to the role you are applying for is very important. Don't forget to also follow the advice I provided earlier in relation to using matching keywords and phrases in your CV from the person specification and job description. The person reading your CV will soon notice these and they are far more likely to offer you an interview if there are similarities between the documents.

Be honest when creating your CV

If you lie on your CV, especially when it comes to academic qualifications or experience, you will almost certainly get caught out at some point in the future. Maybe not straight away, but even a few months or years down the line an employer can still dismiss you for incorrect information that you provide during the selection process. It simply isn't worth it. Be honest when creating your CV and if you don't have the right skills for the job you are applying for, then go out there and get them!

Telephone numbers and answerphones

Think carefully about the contact telephone numbers you leave on your CV.

The first point I want to make is that any number(s) you leave should be from phones that are with you most of the working day. Ideally, you need to be able to answer any calls from prospective employers immediately. However, if an employer needs to leave a message on your answerphone then make sure your answerphone welcome message sounds polite and professional!

Leaving sufficient space on your CV

I have seen many CV's which are cluttered. If I'm honest, I don't usually read them! It is your job to make the employers' job easy when they are reading through your CV. You can achieve this by only including relevant facts on your CV and using sufficient white space. The sample CV's that I included in the previous section are perfect in terms of the amount of white space and their presentation.

Use of font styles and the size of fonts

You do not need to make use of the flashiest and most exotic text fonts in your CV! Again, think about the person reading your CV and the type of image you want to portray. I would imagine that you want to come across as professional and organised and this can be achieved by using fonts such as Arial and Times Roman. I personally choose Arial with a font size of 12 when creating my CV. I also make use of bold headings which are usually size 16.

Use of abbreviations

Unless it is absolutely obvious what the abbreviation is I recommend that you do not use them. The only abbreviations that I feel are appropriate are the ones used for educational qualifications.

The use of 'career breaks'

In an ideal world you will be able to demonstrate a seamless period of employment without career breaks. However, sometimes this is unavoidable, especially if you have taken a career break to raise your family or have been on maternity/paternity leave.

I have seen a few CV's in the past that have given very strange reasons for career breaks, such as:

"To find myself"

"To explore the world with my university friends"

"To take a well-earned break from work"

"To travel"

Whilst there is nothing wrong with any of the above and they are all valid reasons for taking a career break, they could have been written in a better manner. Here's some better ways of explaining career breaks and reasons to include on your CV:

"Travel the world to experience different cultures and languages"

"Time off to study and improve my knowledge and life experiences"

"Time off to look after a relative who had been taken ill"

References – available on request

There is nothing wrong with putting 'References available on request' on your CV; however, I much prefer to see genuine names and contact details of current or previous employers provided as references. It will give an employer more confidence in your abilities to perform the role so I would strongly advise putting down two references on your CV.

The number of previous employment positions can be detrimental

I have to be truthful here, if I see a CV where the applicant has had many different jobs over a relatively short period of time, I will not invite them to interview, regardless of their skills or qualifications. This is simply because if there has already been a history of that person staying in many jobs for a short period of time it is highly likely that they will not stay with my company for a prolonged period of time either. I remember one particular applicant who submitted her CV and she had been through no fewer than 11 jobs in the past 3 years! Personally, I do not want to spend time training up an individual if they are likely to leave soon after. This is also the exact reason why I try to encourage people to stay in a job for at least 12 months at a time; it looks so much better on their CV.

Reasons for leaving

We have all left jobs because we either disliked our boss, our work colleagues or the company we worked for; however, sticking down on your CV you left a post because you 'didn't get on with your boss' is unwise. My advice is simple: do not put down any reasons for leaving your post on your CV unless they are positive ones.

OK, you have now almost reached the end of your guide; I do hope you have found the information helpful. To further assist you in writing an effective CV I have created for you a free online training video and CV templates. You can watch the video and gain access to the CV templates at the following website:

www.CVwritingSkills.co.uk

A FEW FINAL WORDS

You have now reached the end of the guide and no doubt you will be ready to start writing your own CV. Just before you go off and start on your preparation, consider the following.

The majority of candidates who pass any career selection process have a number of common factors. These are as follows:

1. They believe in themselves.

The first factor is self-belief. Regardless of what anyone tells you, you can get to interview and you can pass any career selection process. Just like any job you have to be prepared to work hard in order to be successful. When I left school I achieved very few educational qualifications, but it didn't stop me from achieving what I wanted in life. Make sure you have the self-belief to pass the selection process and fill your mind with positive thoughts.

2. They prepare fully.

The second factor is preparation. Those people who achieve in life prepare fully for every eventuality and that is what you must do when creating your CV or applying for any job application process. Work very hard and especially concentrate on your weak areas.

3. They persevere.

Perseverance is a fantastic word. Everybody comes across obstacles and setbacks in their life, but it is how you react to them that is important. If you fail at something, then ask yourself 'why' have I failed? This will allow you to improve for next time and if you keep improving and trying, success will eventually follow.

4. They are self-motivated.

How much do you want to the particular job you are applying for? Do you want it, or do you really want it? When you apply for a job you should want it more than anything in the world. Your levels of self-motivation will shine through when you walk into the interview and your enthusiasm should come across within your CV.

Finally, don't forget - to further assist you in writing an effective CV I have created for you a free online training video and CV templates. You can watch the video and gain access to the CV templates at the following website:

www.CVwritingSkills.co.uk

Work hard, stay focused and be what you want…

Richard McMun

how2become

Visit www.how2become.com to find more titles and courses that will help you to pass any career selection process, including:

- How to complete job application forms;

- How to pass interviews and assessment centres;

- 1-day career training courses;

- Psychometric testing books and CD's.

www.how2become.com